Thank you for getting our book!

⭐⭐⭐⭐⭐

If you found this book fun and educational, we would be very grateful if you posted a short review on Amazon!

Not long ago, in the sunny city of Fort Worth,
Lee, an athletic and eager boy, rudely kicks the turf.
Yesterday he discovered some very hurtful news:
His parents are divorcing, but he never saw the clues!

Instantly shredding his family's holiday pic, he growls like a prairie dog, oh so quick!

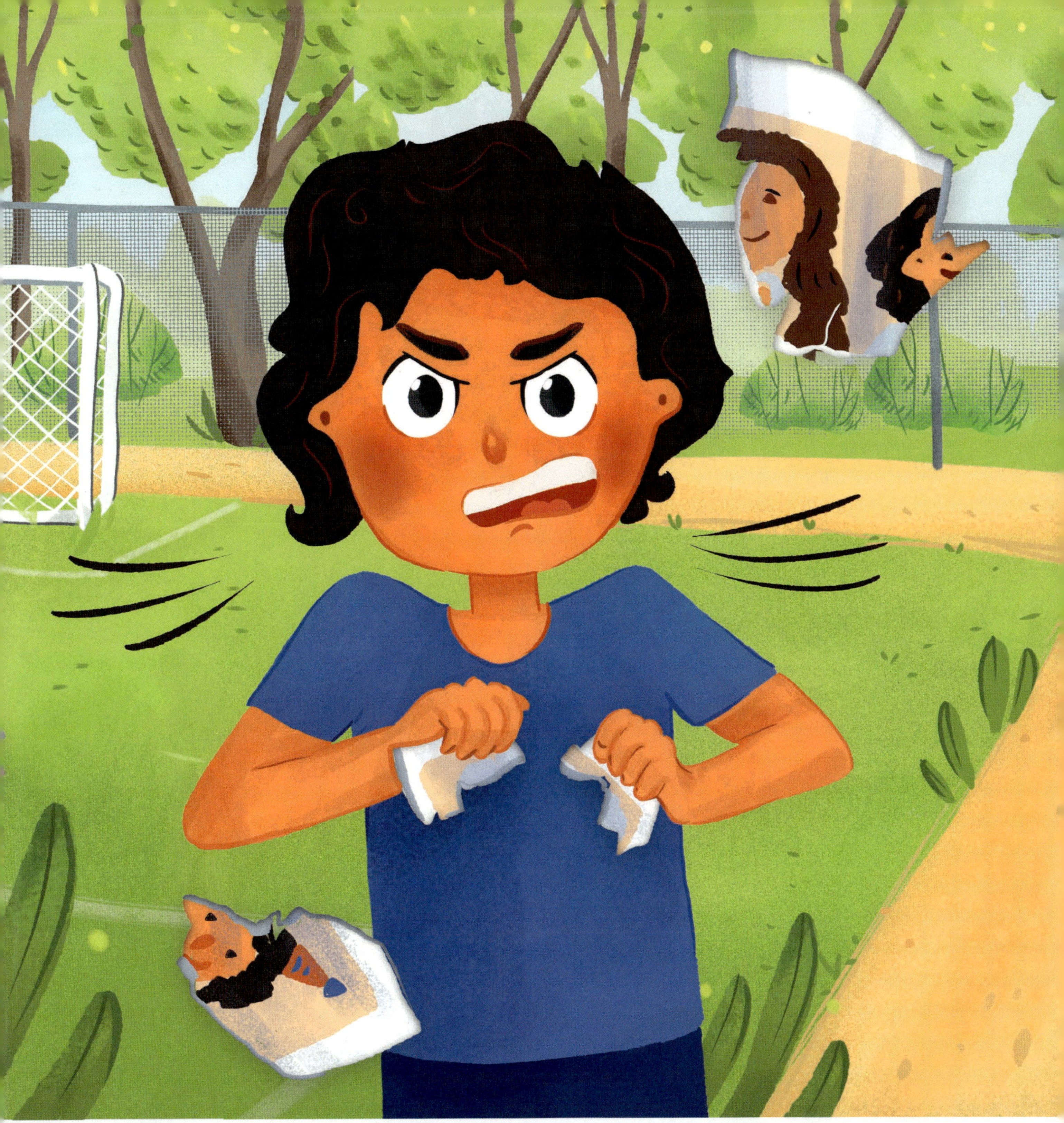

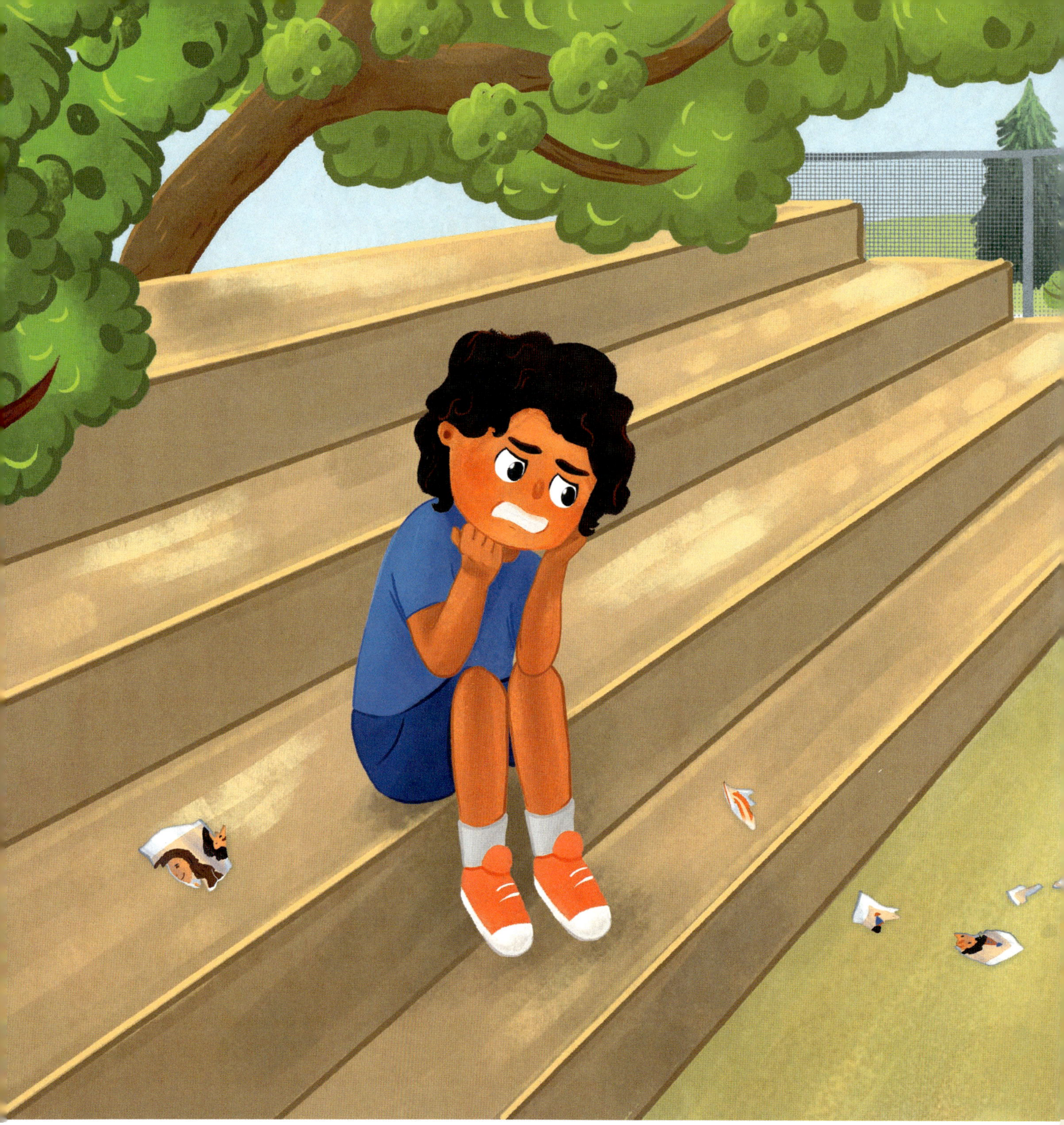

After his scary snarl echoes across the field,
Lee plops onto the bleachers, unable to heal.
He yells, "Why is this happening to me?
They'll ruin my life! Can't they even see?"

Minutes later, Lee freezes at a friendly face:
It's his Coach and P.E. Teacher, Mr. Grace.
Lee really wants to sprint away and just hide.
Coach greets, "Hey!" and sits quietly on the side.

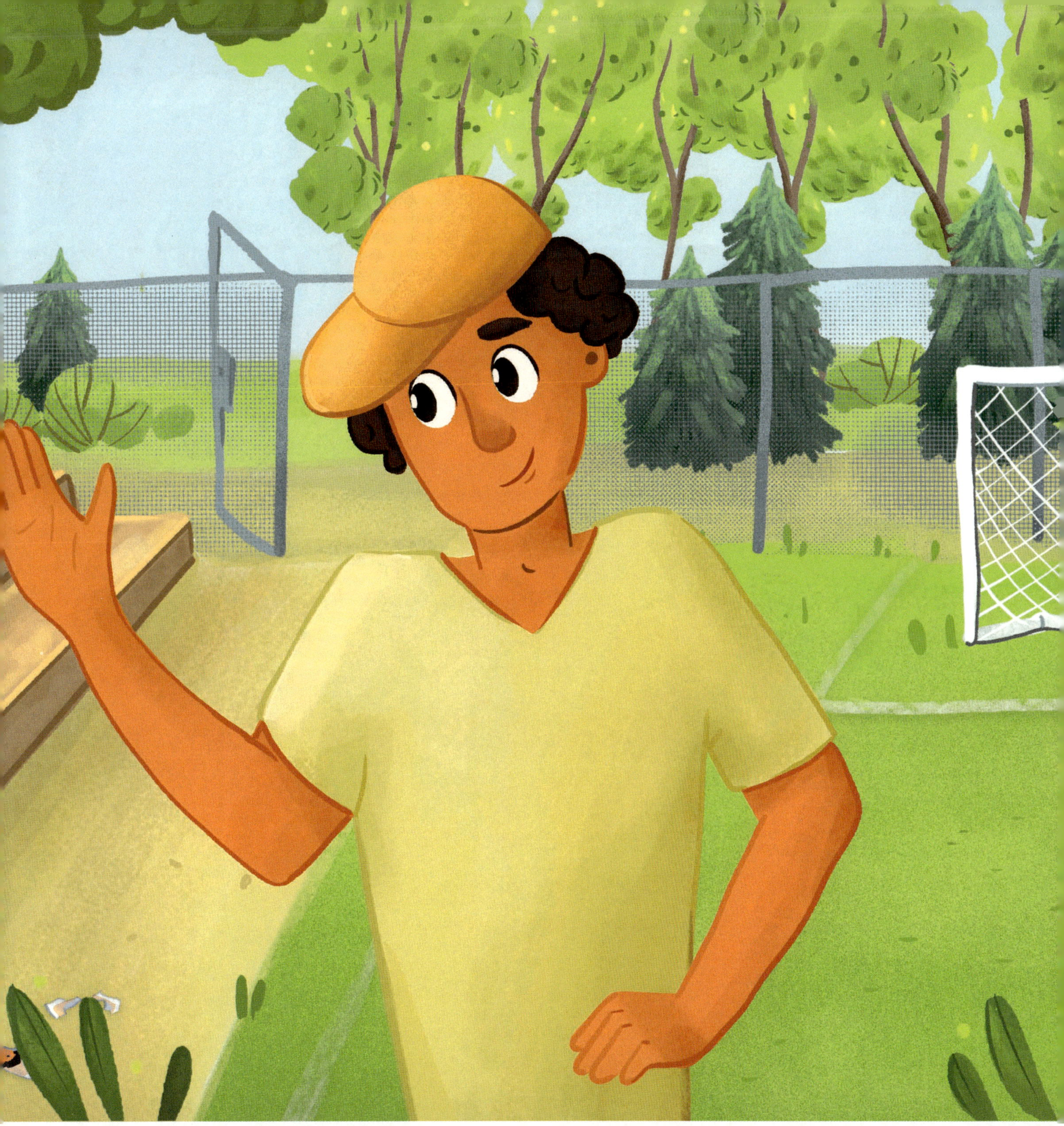

Yet livid Lee stays as silent as a stone.
His heart buzzes; he simply wants to be alone.
But Coach truly cares about Lee like a son.
They've bonded for years and had tons of fun!

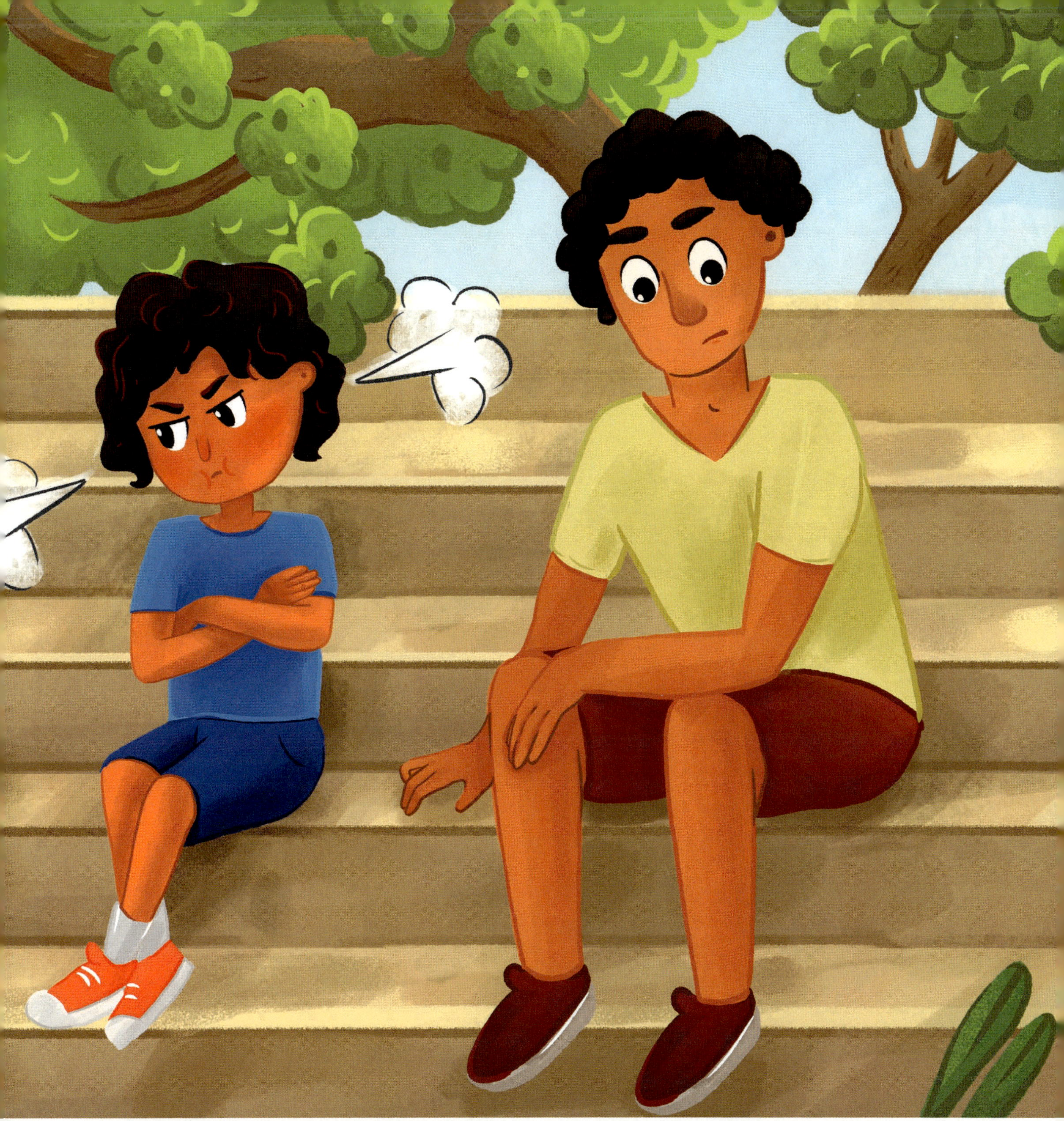

Coach senses that something isn't quite right:
Rage roars in Lee's eyes and his muscles are tight!

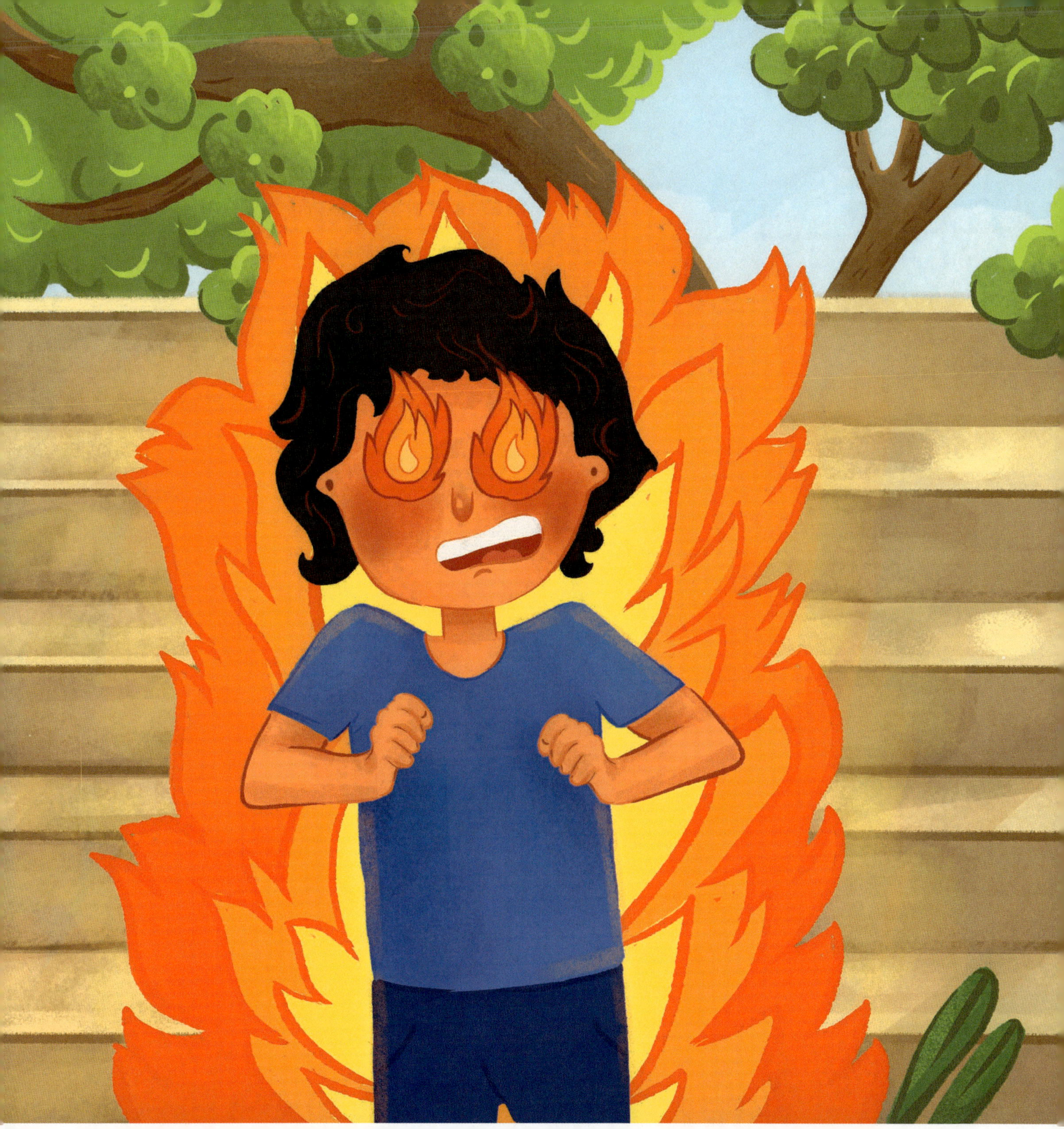

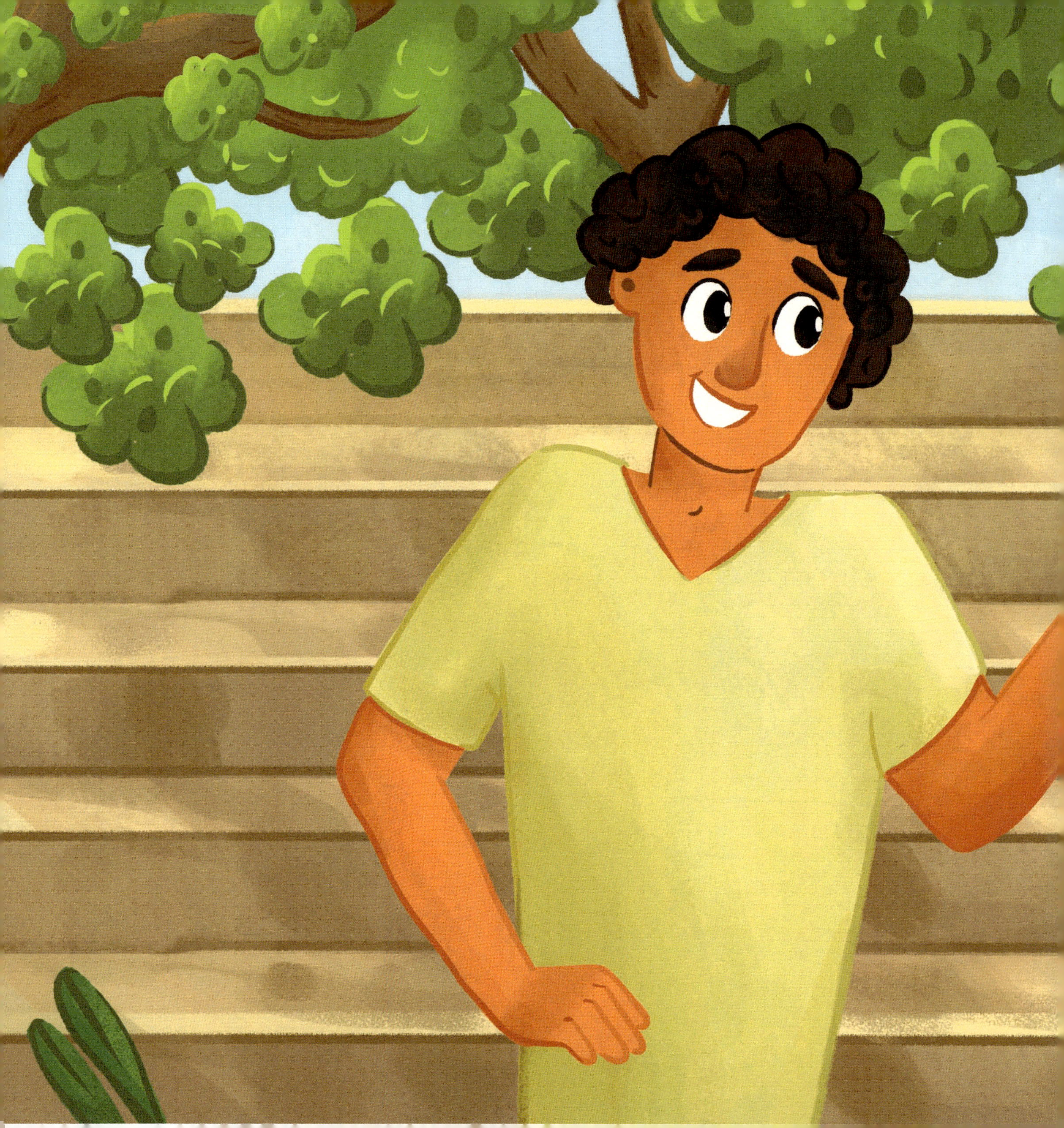

Then Coach grabs a ball and points to Lee:
"Let's toss it around now, just you and me!
I'll share how to release anger using the CALM tip.
Moments later, Lee feels his anger slowly begin to slip.

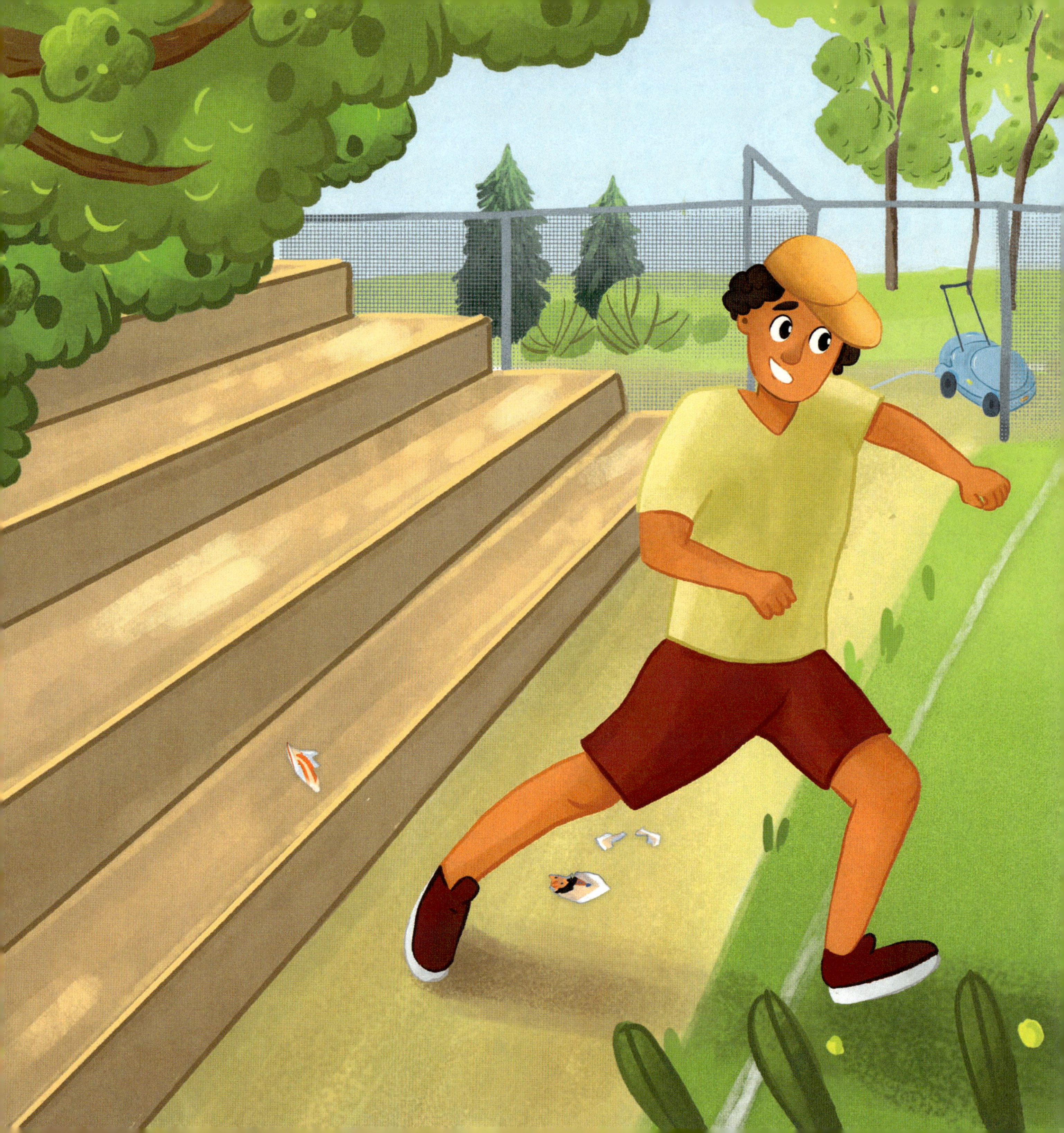

SWOOSHING and swirling the ball like a shooting star,
Lee instantly notices peace, not boiling in fiery, sticky tar!
Coach grins and giggles, "Now feel the C of CALM?
C is for CHANGE your scenery, so your anger doesn't harm!"

After 10 minutes of CHANGING scenery, Lee feels a field of free.
Coach praises, "Add A for fresh AIR: it transforms anger to glee!"
Likewise, Lee's heart rate slows down and his muscles relax.
He exclaims, "No longer do I feel like I'm ready to blow my stack!"

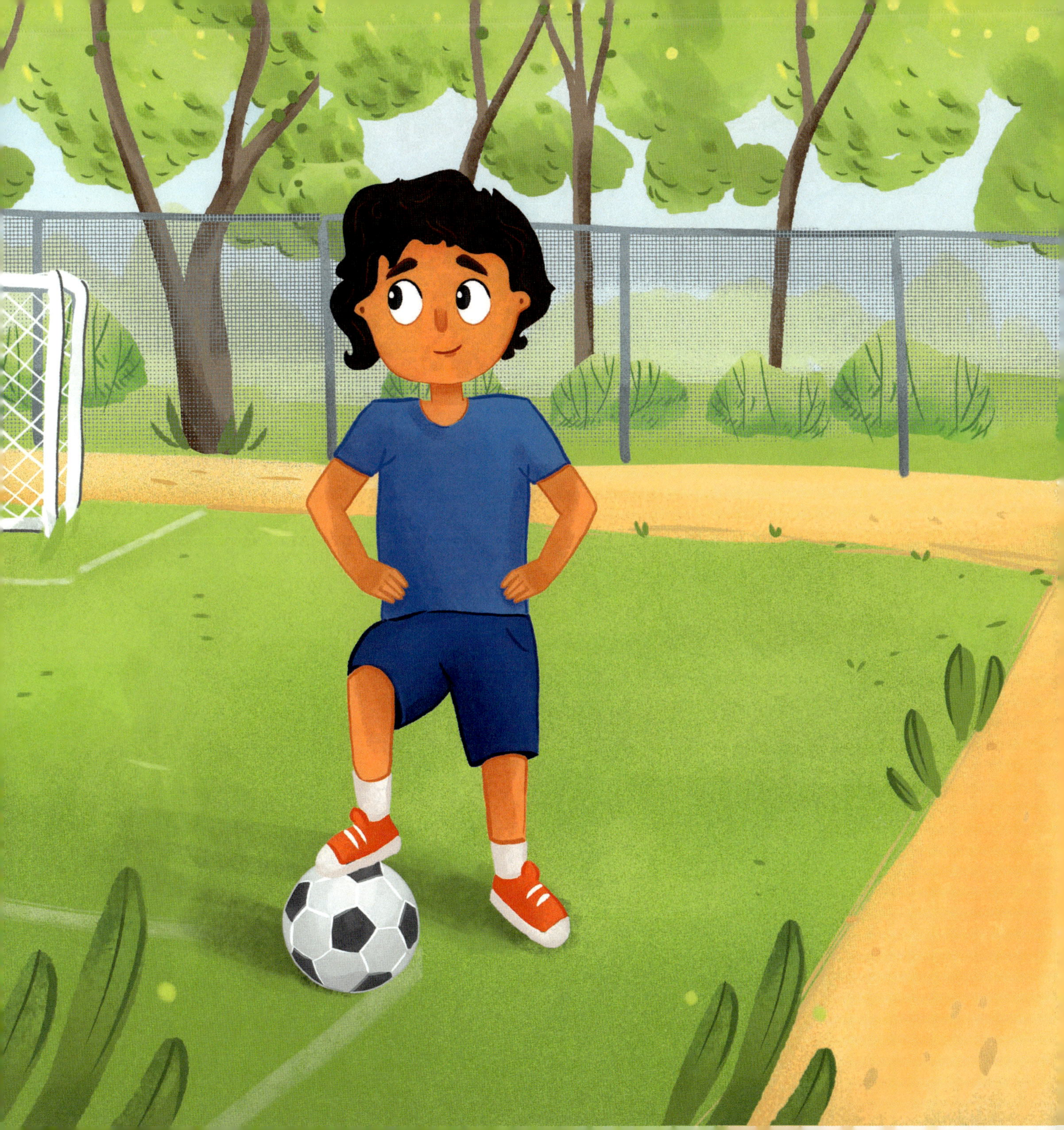

Following the exercise in fresh AIR, Coach finds his folder.
He admits, "Writing and drawing helped me as I grew older!"

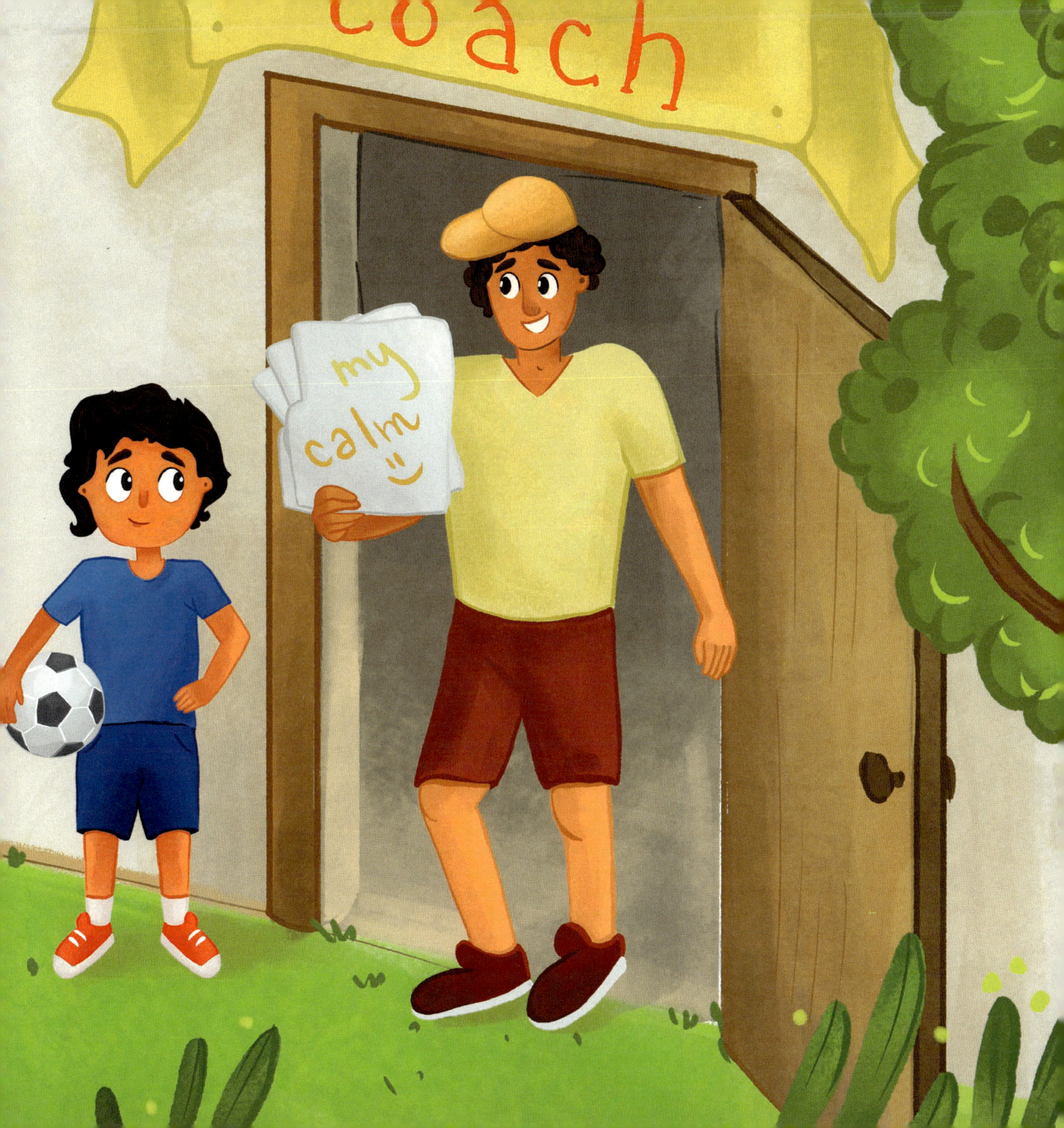
coach
my calm

Coach highlights, "L for Let out feelings in a positive way."
Lee replies, "Maybe I'll pen rap about my angry feelings today!"

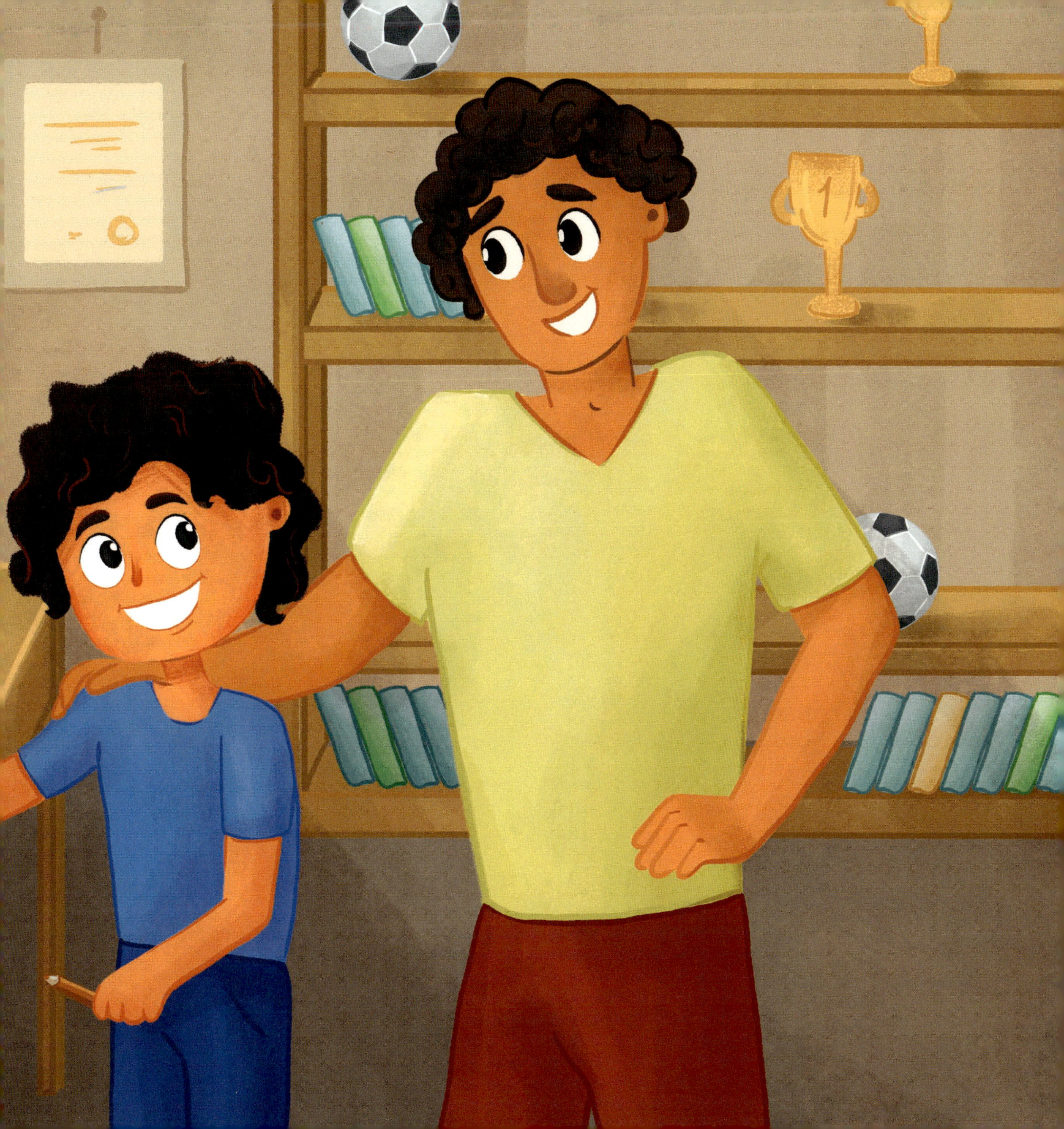

Confidently, Lee reads, "My parents dropped news like a bomb;
But Coach taught me a cool technique, so I can remain CALM!
First, I'll Change up my scenery and inhale some fresh AIR.
Then I'll write, draw, and rap to LET out my feelings with care!"

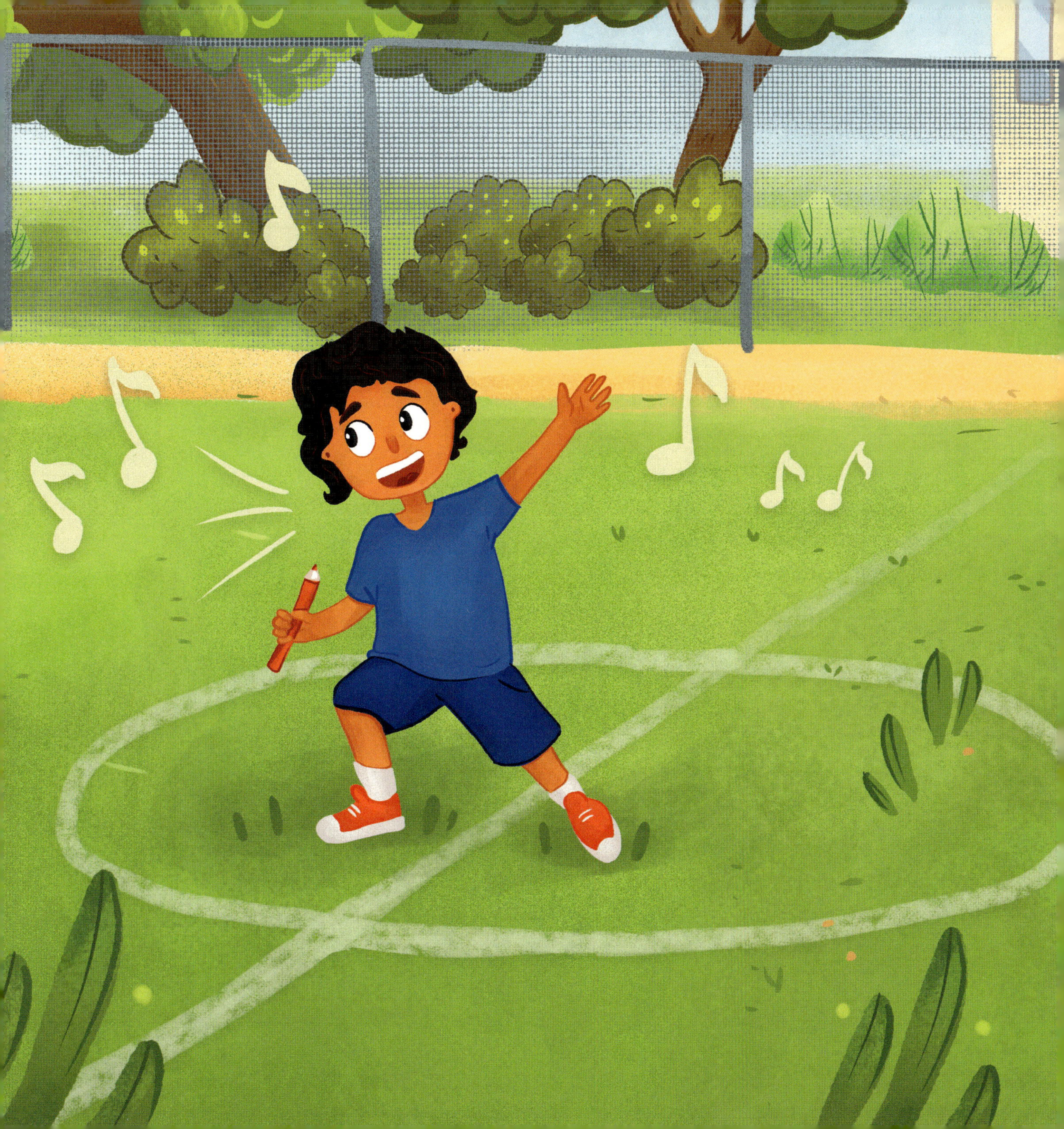

After this victory, Lee glows like a famous halftime star.
To celebrate, Coach busts a move like a crashing car!
As a result of this exercise, Lee joyfully feels in control.
Then Coach rewards him with ice cream: cookie dough in a bowl!

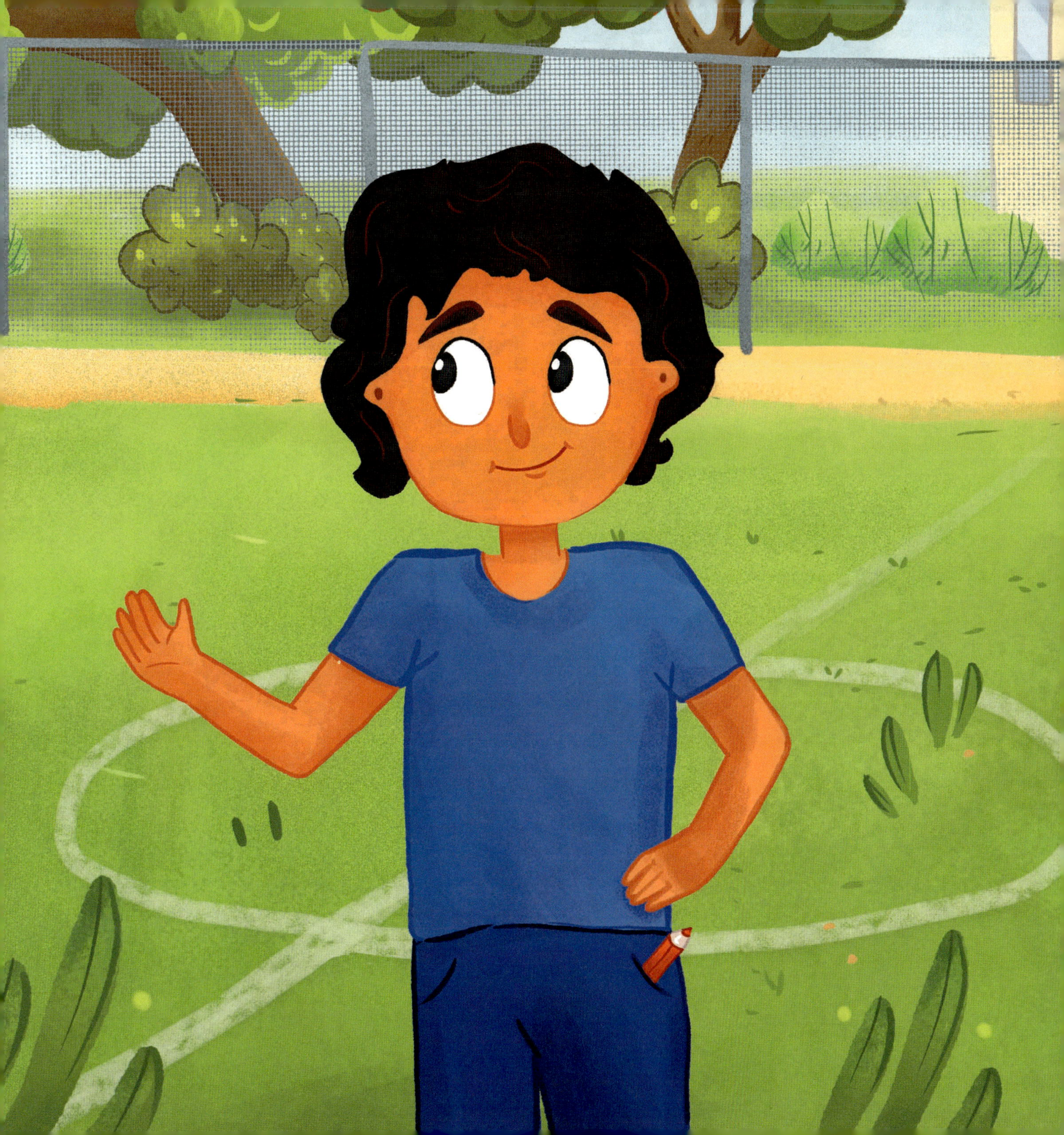

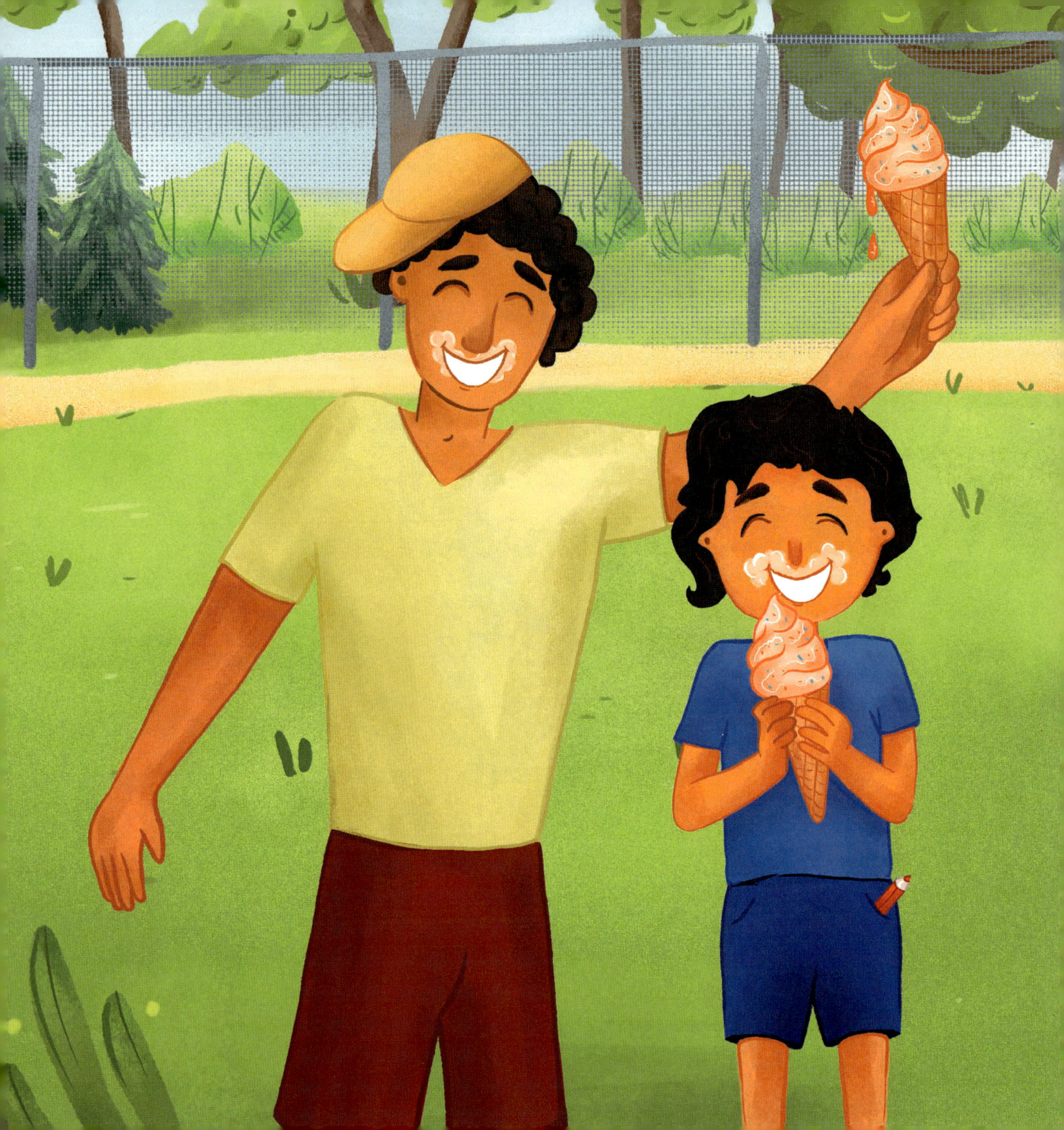

By now, Lee relaxes with his tummy ballooning and full.
He admits, "My parents' divorce jolted me. I acted like a bull!"

So Coach gazes into Lee's sad eyes with lots of respect:
"I know it's hard, Lee, but anger is quite natural to expect."

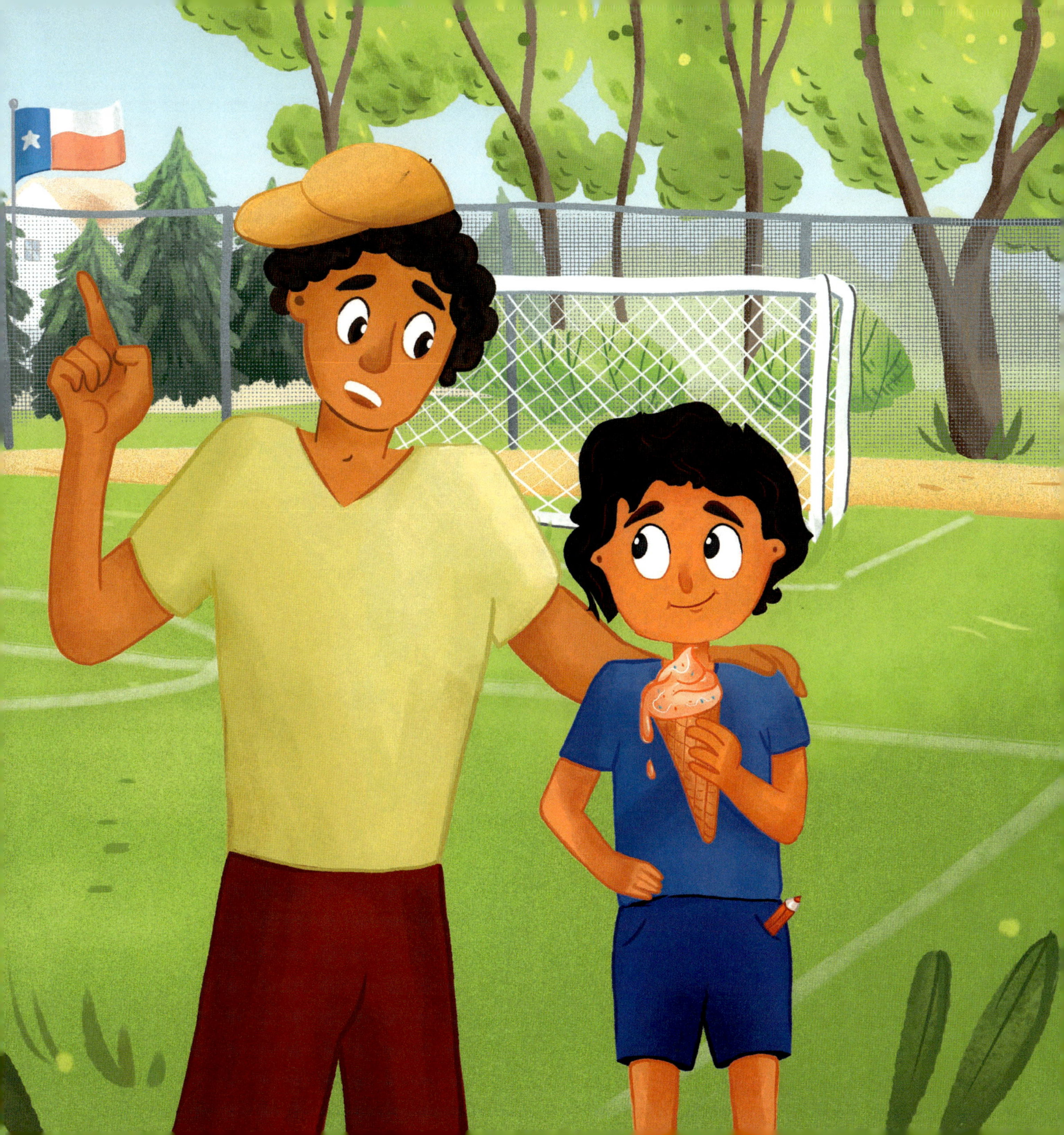

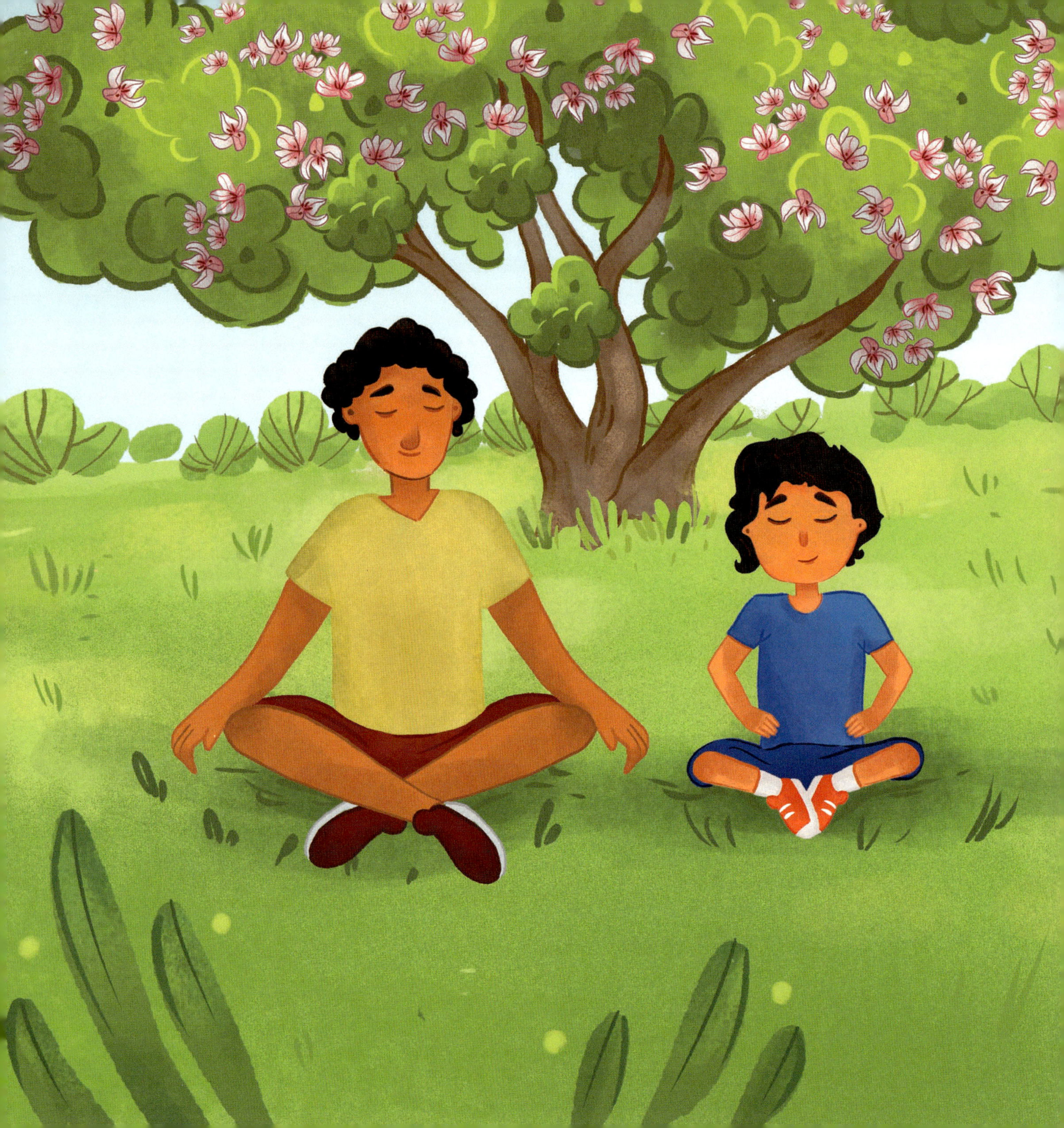

In the end, Lee agrees and vows to not let anger ever win.
Coach guides, "M for MEDITATE while breathing out and in!"
Right away, Lee follows, allowing anger to drift away in the breeze.
They spend the next hour just chatting and admiring the lovely trees.

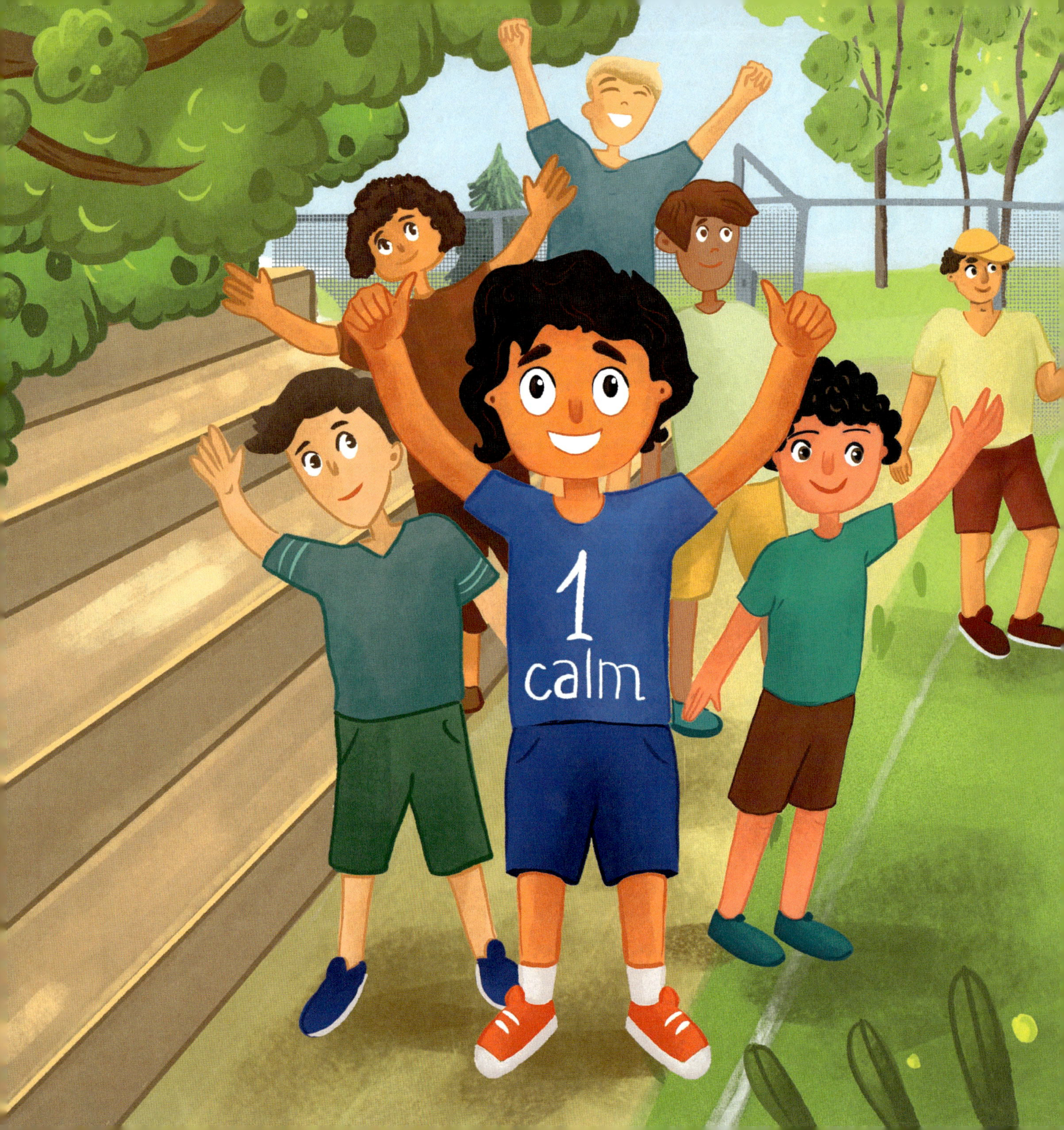
1
calm

Like Lee, you can also play on a field of free!
Try the CALM steps to shift your anger to glee!

Post-Reading Discussions

Running on Rage

Analyze the book's plot and characters. Why was Lee so angry at first? What was the main source of his rage? Why? Be a reading detective!

Lonestar State

Recall the book's setting. With your parents' permission, research 4-8 fun facts about this city and state. Discover what attractions are there, the history, the population, the climate, and other useful information. Explore U.S. geography today!

Stealth Health

Scan the book and jot down 2-5 anger signs that Lee showed with his body, words, gestures, actions, and face. What signs do you tend to exhibit when you're angry? Do a body scan the next time you're upset and get stealth health!

Life Strife

The author knows that life isn't always easy. What type of challenges, big emotions, and problems do you face at home or school? Make a list of 4-8 common ones and/or draw what triggers your anger. Let art and writing heal your strife!

Change It Up

Use the C in the CALM technique today. When you're frustrated, sad, or mad, walk to another room, set down a yoga mat on your porch or patio, read a book to enter a new setting, or just go to a quiet place in your home to think. Be mindful today!

Coach Grace	Imagine that it's 10 years after the book. Create a thank you card for Coach Grace from Lee. How did the CALM technique help him through life? Be creative.
Air For Mindful Flair	Lee notices how A for fresh Air calmed him and made him more mindful. Create a list of 4-8 activities in fresh air (and/or that promote air and oxygen) that you can do when you're mad. For example, a. I can take a walk with my dad in the fresh air on the local trail with my dog.
Write Stuff	Both Lee and Coach use writing and art to release or L Let out feelings. Devise a poem, story, drawing, collage, rap, song, cheer, play, or puppet show about something that made you angry. Let writing and art free the flames of anger in you! Explore those ELA skills!
Meditate Against Hate	Pick any line, word, affirmation, mantra, poem, or quote that will let your mind, body, and soul free to M for Meditate while breathing out and in against anger and hate. For instance, I like to recite, "Peace begins with me!" or "This, too, shall pass!" Practice synching your meditation with your deep breathing, in and out. Reflect on how you feel repeating a few times. Mend anger with meditation and mindfulness!
Animal Anger	State the animal simile used by the author to compare Lee's anger at the beginning of the book. A simile is a figure of speech that compares to things using "like" or "as." Finally, draw which animal you represent when you're calm. Practice similes for ELA success!

Thank you
for getting our book!

⭐⭐⭐⭐⭐

If you found this book fun and educational, we would be very grateful if you posted a short review on Amazon! Your support does make a difference and we read every review personally.

If you would like to leave a review, just head on over to this book's Amazon page and click "Write a customer review".

Thank you for your support!

⭐⭐⭐⭐⭐

Manufactured by Amazon.ca
Bolton, ON